ESTABLISHED 1840.

J. G. ROBINSON &

General and Furnishing Ir ......

Gasfitters, Locksmiths and Bellhangers,

92 GRANGE ROAD, AND 54 MARKET STREET, BIRKENHEAD.

Best Goods at Moderate Prices.   Competent Workmen kept on the Premises.

TRADE MARK.

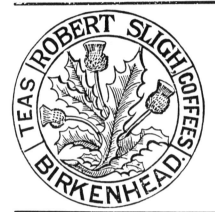

CHOICE
TEAS AND COFFEES
For Family Use.

231 GRANGE ROAD
CHARING CROSS.

E. SUTTON
Wholesale & Retail Butcher
166 GRANGE ROAD
BIRKENHEAD.

ALL ORDERS PUNCTUALLY ATTENDED TO.

WOODWARD & CAVE
GROCERS. TEA & COFFEE DEALERS
PROVISION MERCHANTS,
256 GRANGE ROAD, CHARING CROSS.

Our Prices will bear favourable comparison to any other House in the Trade.

Branches—83 and 264 OLD CHESTER ROAD.

BIRKENHEAD
A Pictorial History

A 1920s comic postcard from Birkenhead

BIRKENHEAD
A Pictorial History

Ian Boumphrey

Phillimore

1995

Published by
PHILLIMORE & CO. LTD.
Shopwyke Manor Barn, Chichester, West Sussex

ISBN 0 85033 988 X

Printed and bound in Great Britain by
BIDDLES LTD.
Guildford, Surrey

List of Illustrations

Frontispiece: A comic postcard, 1920s

Acknowledgements

I am grateful to the following people who have loaned their photographs and/or supplied me with information:

Birkenhead School Archives, 35,139,140,141; Peter Bowskill; Mrs Mary Davies, 165,166; Peter Denye, 54; Bill Johnstone, 112; Norman Lenox, 37,117,118,177; His Honour Judge McKay, M.A., 80,81,82; Rosemary Tilleard-Lewis, 142; and staff at Birkenhead Central Library. I would especially like to thank Albert Nute for his research and advice, and all the other people, too many to mention, that contributed in any way towards this publication.

Introduction

Birkenhead is situated in the North East of the Wirral Peninsula, which was in Norman times and earlier covered mainly with woods but with stretches of heathland and some swampy areas. This pictorial history of Birkenhead takes the reader through from Victorian times to the 1950s. It is said that Birkenhead derived its name from either the old Norse words 'birch' and 'hefod'—meaning the headland of birches, or from its position at the head of the river Birken or Birket. Hence Woodside gained its name during these early days of Birkenhead. To learn of the area's background, we go back to about 1150 when a Norman baron, Hamo de Mascy of Dunham, who owned considerable land in Wirral, founded a Benedictine priory, dedicated to the Blessed Virgin Mary and St James which was sited on a headland overlooking the river Mersey. The ruins are still there and open to the public. The Chapter House has served as a chapel since the dissolution and, following the demolition of St Mary's Church 1820-1975, continues in use today. In addition to the priory, the monks had a farm on the area now covered by Alfred Road and Grange Mount. The route connecting the farm and priory was known as Grange Lane (now Grange Road).

The monks gave hospitality to travellers and ferried people across the river. In 1275 King Edward I first stayed at the priory, and then again two years later, when he was preparing a campaign against the Welsh.

Because increasing numbers of people wanted to cross the river, the monks successfully petitioned Edward II, requesting permission to provide houses as lodgings at the ferry, and to sell food there. In 1330, Edward III was petitioned by the monks for the sole right to ferry passengers to Liverpool, and to charge tolls. A Royal Charter was granted and this is commemorated on a tapestry in the Williamson Art Gallery and Museum. The charter stated that

> the Prior and the Convent and their successors for ever may have there [at the Priory], a passage beyond the arm of the sea, as well as for men as for horses, and other things whatsoever, and for the same passage may receive as shall be deemed reasonable.

As more of the forest was given over to cultivation, so the people of Wirral had more produce to sell and, with a ready demand across the Mersey, the ferry over to Liverpool's weekly market became more popular. The prior and monks also increased output from their own land and eventually built a granary in Water Street, Liverpool, in which to store their corn, to be sold at the Liverpool Market.

The priory and the area around it changed very little for the next two centuries. However, because of Henry VIII's dissolution of the monasteries, the priory was closed in 1536. The priory estates were bought from the crown in 1544 by Ralph Worsley of Lancashire, a former page at court, for £568 11s. 6d.—seemingly a bargain! The ownership passed to Thomas Powell, who had married Worsley's daughter, and it remained in the Powell family until c.1710, when it was purchased by a Liverpool merchant, John Cleveland.

The tolls about this time were: passengers 1d.; cheese 1s. a ton; man and horse 6d.; sheep 4d. a score; cows 3d.; sacks 1d. each; butcher's horse 4d.; baskets and parcels free. This tells us much about the traffic crossing the Mersey at this time.

Upon John Cleveland's death in 1716, the estates passed to his daughter, Alice, who married Francis Price of Flintshire, and they then remained in the Price family, who lived at the Hall close to the priory, for the next 150 years.

By the mid-18th century, the population around the priory on the headland had not increased to any great extent. Even so, the ferry traffic was becoming busier despite the poor condition of the connecting roads. In 1762, a six-horsed coach ran from Woodside to Chester and Parkgate three days a week, taking the route via the present Grange Road, Whetstone Lane, Church Road (Tranmere) and then joining the Old Chester Road by Dacre Hill. An important date was 1787 when the Old Chester Road was made into a turnpike road and became a main highway. This increased the traffic using the crossing to Liverpool, but did little to increase the population of what was then the beginnings of Birkenhead and, by the turn of the century, the townships of Tranmere, Oxton and Bidston had greater populations than that of Birkenhead which at that time had 110 people living there. By 1810, the population had fallen to 105 and had only risen to 200 by 1821. However, that was all to change over the next fifty years.

Across the Mersey in Liverpool by 1800 there was a population of 79,000. Trade was rapidly increasing, bringing crowded and noisy streets and, although new docks and warehouses were being built, they could not keep up with demand.

Back in Birkenhead, St Mary's Church, in the old priory grounds, was completed in 1821 and, because of the improved steam ferry service crossing the river, Birkenhead had begun to develop in this area around Church Street.

The arrival in 1824 of William Laird, who in 1810 had come from Scotland to Liverpool, was one of the main factors in changing the face of Birkenhead over the following decades. He purchased a piece of land on Wallasey Pool, at the end of Cleveland Street, to build his shipyard, which was to become famous worldwide over the next 150 years. In 1829, they built their first iron vessel and, in 1833, their first paddle steamer.

Mr. Laird did not devote all his energies to shipbuilding, for he also inspired the building of Hamilton Square (named after his mother's family) and the plan for broad streets which spread inland from the square.

By 1831, the population of Birkenhead had increased to 2,569 and, due to this, two years later, an Act was passed for the appointment of 'Commissioners for the improvement of Birkenhead'. Their responsibilities included paving, lighting, watching, cleansing, regulation of the police and establishing a market. In July 1835, both the first town hall and the market were opened, adjoining each other in Hamilton Street; the police station was situated in the town hall building. In 1835, yet another ferry was started— at Monks Ferry sited between the original Woodside Ferry and Birkenhead Ferry to the south. The latter had started to operate in 1820 and closed in 1870. The new Monks Ferry service initially lasted only two years as it had not been legally sanctioned, but it restarted in 1845 when a tunnel extension on the new Chester railway line was completed with a station that linked the trains and boats.

The Birkenhead and Chester Railway, which had its terminus at Grange Lane, was opened in 1840. This was bad news for the *Woodside Hotel* which had been built only six years previously to cater for the increasing number of coaches for the ferry trade; it was said to have stabling for 100 horses. The new railway proved much faster and more convenient, except initially when the terminus was at Grange Lane. Monks ferry and station closed in 1878 when Woodside station was opened.

In 1841, the population had risen to 8,223 but the adjoining villages had not increased at the same rate. It was announced in the same year that the tolls on the ferry were to be increased, but the Birkenhead Commissioners came to the rescue and in 1842 leased the ferryage, with its exclusive rights of ferry from Birkenhead to Liverpool, which they then purchased in 1858. About this time it was estimated that two million passengers annually crossed on the Woodside ferry, as well as an undisclosed number of cattle and pigs in addition to milk and produce for the Liverpool markets. Two of Laird's iron ships—the *Prince* and *Queen*—were then the largest and fastest used on this service which also included the *Nun*, the *Eliza Price*, the *Cleveland* and the *Kingfisher* (the latter two were not Laird's vessels).

In 1843, the township of Claughton-cum-Grange and part of Oxton were incorporated with Birkenhead. The same year, the Commissioners purchased some 226 acres of swampy land. They engaged Joseph Paxton to turn it into a beautiful park of 125 acres, which was officially opened in 1847 by Lord Morpeth in conjunction with the docks; the balance of the land was sold for surrounding residential development. The Birkenhead Commissioners built a new market in 1845, to supply the demand from a growing population, which by 1851 had increased to 24,285 and by 1861 had reached 35,929.

Meanwhile, Wallasey Pool, where William Laird had built his shipyard, was ideal when the tide was in, but became a narrow stream when the tide was out. The potential of building a port and docks at Birkenhead was soon realised when the port of Liverpool was unable to cope with its increasing traffic. Therefore, an engineer was engaged to design a dam across the mouth of the pool, to build a low water basin and to construct two docks. On 23 October 1844, the foundation stone of the docks was laid by Viscount Egerton and on 5 April 1847 the new Morpeth and Egerton Docks were opened by Lord Morpeth. One of the problems when the docks were built was that ships at Laird's were no longer able to be launched into Wallasey Pool. So land between Birkenhead Ferry and Monk's Ferry was chosen as the new site for Laird's shipyard. Then in 1858, the Mersey Docks and Harbour Board took over the dock estate and over the years improved the facilities. The original scheme of an entrance to the float from a low water basin (open to the river) was abandoned and the basin was converted into the Alfred Dock with three locked entrances into the river, opened in 1866.

On the education front, according to *White's Directory* for 1850, a university was planned for Birkenhead as it was felt there was a need for such an institution in the North of England and it was intended to be devoted to the same ideals as the old-established universities of Oxford and Cambridge. Five acres of land were purchased for the college on a ridge just within the township of 'Claughton-cum-Birkenhead' with the site commanding extensive views over the peninsula. The collegiate buildings were planned to be built around an inner quadrangle, and were to be in the Tudor style of architecture of about 1500. The front and the dressings were to be of Storeton stone and the inner of Flaybrick and Storeton stone. The estimated cost was about £20,000 with the Archbishop of Canterbury, the Marquis of Westminster and Lord Robert Grosvenor each contributed £1,000 towards this plan, but nothing came of it.

The 1860s started with the town having the first public tramway system in Europe. This was a new idea from an American, Francis Train, and the line ran from Woodside Ferry along Argyle Street and Conway Street to the Birkenhead Park entrance. The service, which proved to be very successful, opened on 20 August 1860.

In 1861, John Laird, son of William, became the first Member of Parliament for Birkenhead, with Claughton, Oxton, Tranmere and part of Bebington, and, to commemorate this, he funded the building of Birkenhead Borough Hospital in Park Road North, which opened in 1863. Also in 1861, a floating landing stage with connecting bridge was moored at Woodside and in the same year the Birkenhead Board of Guardians of the poor was established. Its first action was to build the Birkenhead Institution in Church Road, Tranmere (now St Catherine's Hospital) which accommodated 629 inmates.

In 1862, the American Confederate Commerce Raider *Alabama* was built by Laird. This ship caused great damage to the trade of the Union States until she was sunk in 1864. Together with other raiders, this vessel cost Britain £3 million in damages which were awarded to the United States by an International Court in 1873.

On 23 April 1864, Birkenhead's first purpose-built public library was opened in Hamilton Street, the library having been housed, since 1856, in a reading room in Price Street. Then, in 1857, the library had been moved to rooms over the new post office in Conway Street.

The year 1866 saw the opening of the Birkenhead-Hoylake Railway, which took over most of the trade from the coach and horses which had run from the *Green Lodge Hotel*, Hoylake to the *Woodside Hotel*.

As an indication of the strong religious feelings of mid-Victorian times reference should be made to two riots at Birkenhead. The first, in 1849, arose because of a Protestant protest meeting at the town hall, following the establishment of a Roman Catholic hierarchy and episcopate in England. The Catholics, led by a great number of Irish navvies engaged in the docks, broke the windows of the town hall and disrupted the meeting, the police being heavily outnumbered. A further open-air meeting was held at the end of the year with a strong police and military presence.

In 1862, when Garibaldi was visiting Britain, a Protestant debating society held a meeting sympathetic to the Italian patriot at Holy Trinity Church School. Echoing troubles in London, a Catholic mob attacked the lecture room, causing the meeting to be abandoned. The local priest eventually induced the mob to disperse, although claiming a 'victory'. When the meeting was reconvened a week later, a large force of special constables plus county police and troops, some from Manchester, was mustered. As the police and special constables were positioned defensively round the building, the mob turned to pillaging shops and public houses. Damage estimated at £3,000 was done, largely due to the failure of the Magistrates to act decisively (even with troops present) as had also been the case in 1849. On both occasions the chairman was Sir Edward Cust of Leasowe Castle.

By 1871, the population had grown to 42,997 and with this had come industrial and commercial development together with churches, and theatres. In this year, the Laird School of Art opened in Park Road North, which was a further gift to the town from John Laird. In 1874, Birkenhead mourned the death of John Laird (son of William), who had done so much for the development of Birkenhead. On the day of his funeral, work stopped in the town to see the cortège attended by 1,500 of the men who normally worked at the shipyard who walked behind the funeral carriages. His two sons, John and William, carried on his good work, serving Birkenhead.

On 13 August 1877, the Charter of Incorporation was granted and Birkenhead became a borough. This embraced the whole of the Township of Birkenhead and included the districts of Claughton, Oxton, Tranmere and part of the Township and

District of Higher Bebington. The first elections took place on 14 November 1877 with the first mayor being John Laird (son of John Laird, the first M.P.).

The following year, 1878, Woodside station was opened, which finally linked the railway with the major ferry crossing. This made the Monk's Ferry station and ferry redundant and they were then closed down. This year also saw the opening of the Wirral Tramway from Woodside to New Ferry.

By 1881, the population of the borough had risen to 84,006 within its enlarged boundaries and was still growing; more houses and public buildings were being built. On 21 June 1883, the Birkenhead Children's Hospital in Woodchurch Road was officially opened by the Duke of Westminster. In 1903 a large extension was made to the hospital including a new out-patients' department.

Proposals for a road tunnel under the Mersey had been put before Liverpool Corporation in 1827 and 1830, both initiated by Cheshire interests but not pursued. It was not until the early 1880s that work started on a rail tunnel which was officially opened on 20 January 1886 by the Prince of Wales (later Edward VII). The gloom in the tunnel and the smell from the steam trains made the journey unpleasant. Despite this, the route proved popular with businessmen who could work in Liverpool and live on the other side of the Mersey, in Wirral.

The following year was a landmark in Birkenhead's history, when on 10 February 1887 the Town Hall was opened. It was built of Storeton stone at a cost £43,067 and overlooked Hamilton Square, whose elegant buildings had been completed by the 1850s. The private gardens in the centre of the square were bought by the Town Council in 1903 and opened to the public.

The population continued to grow and by 1891 had reached 99,857. The Church schools were unable to cope with the growing number of children, so a School Board was formed in 1893. The Woodlands School was then opened in 1895, followed in the next few years by Cathcart Street, Laird Street and Well Lane schools. In 1903, the School Board was superseded by the Education Committee of the Borough.

Like any town of its size, Birkenhead had problems with poverty and in 1892 Charles Thompson, a Birkenhead grocer, opened a Poor Children's Mission in the premises of a former Quakers' Meeting House in Hemingford Street which aimed to cope with outcasts of society of all ages and especially with children. Although he died in 1903, his daughter, Annie, took over as superintendent, continuing until she died in the 1960s. Their work is still carried on today.

Birkenhead had had a gas supply since 1840 and the Corporation was one of the first authorities to provide electricity when, in 1896, they supplied the town from a generating station on a site between Craven Street and Bentinck Street. Another generating station was built in Craven Street which supplied the new electric trams, which started operating from February 1901, initially on the Woodside to New Ferry route. It was in this year that the Town Hall clock tower was rebuilt after being destroyed by fire in July. The population had, by then, increased to 110,915. In 1903, Laird's merged with the Sheffield steel manufacturer Charles Cammell & Co. Ltd. to become Cammell Laird & Co. Ltd.

The last horse-drawn trams operated in Birkenhead in 1903, the same year that travelling by rail to Liverpool became a lot more comfortable after 3 May, when the Electric Railway was opened. Following increased demand from a growing population, the new G.P.O. building was opened in Argyle Street in 1907. This replaced the post office building in Conway Street. The Vittoria Dock was opened in 1909, to help cope with the increased trade and, by 1911, the population had grown to 130,794.

By 1913, the tramcar fleet had reached its maximum total of 68, providing the town with a very adequate service. The following year saw plans to introduce motor buses, but this was postponed due to the First World War; the first service finally opened on 12 July 1919 on the Park station to Rock Ferry route.

The population had increased to 147,577 by 1921 and in this year, on 15 August, the long-awaited water scheme was inaugurated with the borough being supplied from the Olwen Reservoir in North Wales.

The borough boundaries were extended in 1928, to include Thingwall, Landican, Prenton and parts of Bidston. In the same year the Williamson Art Gallery and Museum opened, and after the widening and deepening of the river entrances was completed, the Alfred Dock lock entrance was opened by Lord Derby.

Over the years, in addition to Birkenhead Park, various other areas for recreation were provided by the Council: Thurstaston Common, outside the town boundaries, in 1881; Mersey Park in Tranmere in 1885; Bidston Hill, helped by public subscription, in 1894 and 1908; Victoria Park, Tranmere, in 1901 and the Arno, Oxton, in 1912. Arrowe Park on the western boundary of the town was acquired from Lord Leverhulme in 1927. It was here that the World Scout Jamboree was held. It opened on 31 July 1929 and for the next fortnight it was host to 50,000 scouts from all over the world.

The population by 1931 was 147,946 and the borough boundaries were extended again in 1933 to include Noctorum, Woodchurch and parts of Arrowe, Bidston and Upton. The same year saw the opening of Byrne Avenue Baths and the extension of the docks, when Bidston Dock was opened on 28 April.

The growth of motorised transport after the First World War meant that the goods ferry services across the Mersey were unable to cope adequately with this increased traffic. A committee was set up in 1922 which decided that a tunnel crossing would be more practical than a bridge, and this culminated in work on building the Mersey Road Tunnel in December 1925. The tunnel, which measured 2.13 miles between the Birkenhead and Liverpool main entrances, took over eight years to complete and cost £7,723,000. It was opened by King George V and Queen Mary on 18 July 1934, the same day that they opened the new library in Borough Road. This replaced the library donated by Andrew Carnegie, which had been opened in 1909 but had had to be demolished to make way for the new tunnel entrance.

The end of an era came when, after serving the people of Birkenhead faithfully for 77 years, the last tramcar service operated in the town. The horse-drawn tramcars had been replaced with electric ones in 1901 but, due to the flexibility of the buses, which had caused all but one tram service to close, and the rundown state of the trams, they finally ceased operating on 17 July 1937, when the Oxton Circle route was closed.

This was the same year that the *Ark Royal* was launched from Cammell Laird's shipyard and she was fitted out just in time to join in hostilities, after war had broken out on 3 September 1939. The late 1930s was a busy time for Cammell Laird; the largest merchant ship of the time to be built in England, the *Mauretania,* was launched in 1938, to be followed a year later by the battleship *Prince of Wales*. During the Second World War, Cammell Laird built 106 fighting ships and carried out repairs on over 2,000 ships of all types.

It is significant that we end with Cammell Laird for, without the Laird family's business and generosity, Birkenhead would never have developed into the town we know today. It is sad to note that Cammell Laird's shipyard closed down in 1993.

1 The 'Grant of Arms' of the Borough of Birkenhead is dated 28 August 1878. The Pastoral Staff and the Lion formed part of the Seal of the Tranmere Local Board. The motto translates: 'Where there is faith there is also light and strength'. This is depicted in the crest by the cross and crozier suggesting Faith; the star and crescent, Light and the oaks & lions, Strength.

2 The Birkenhead Priory Chapter House, which dates back to *c.*1150 and is pictured here in 1904, is the oldest building in Birkenhead and surrounding area. It was Hammo de Massey who founded the monastery here which was run by Benedictine monks, the first recorded inhabitants of Birkenhead. The Chapter House is still used today as a place of worship.

3 The remains of the northern and western elevations of the Guest Hall of Birkenhead Priory are seen here in the 1930s. The Guest Hall was built *c.*1270 and was used by the monks to entertain important guests, including Edward I, who visited here in 1275 and 1277. The spire in the background is that of St Mary's Parish Church (*see* plate 4).

4 St Mary's Parish Church was consecrated on 17 December 1821, having been built by the Lord of the Manor, Francis Price, at his own expense. It was erected on land adjoining Birkenhead Priory, where the chapel had become too small for worshippers. The church flourished until the 1960s when the houses in the vicinity were demolished to make way for the Mersey Tunnel approaches. The church was closed in 1970 and demolished in the mid-1970s, with only the spire and part of the walls remaining.

5 Over the years, Birkenhead has supplied many men for the armed forces. Sergeant J.A. Stubbs, Recruiting Sergeant, is seen standing at the entrance to the Admiralty Recruiting Office at 74 Chester Street prior to the First World War. A poster advertising the Royal Marines is seen to the right of the boy 'recruit'. This part of Chester Street was demolished in the 1960s (*see* plate 4).

6 Looking down Waterloo Place from Chester Street in 1904, the pub on the left is the *Prince Alfred* and on the right is the *Shakespeare Hotel*. Many of the houses beyond are lodgings advertised at 4d (2p) per night. This street was the scene of a murder in 1894 when John Murphy, who lodged at No. 2, on the right, died following a street fight. The attacker received one month's imprisonment for manslaughter.

7 & 8 The properties in these two photographs are further down Waterloo Place, seen in the previous picture. These are the front views of nos.21 and 25, which were built in the 1850s and are seen here in 1904. Both properties are in an obvious state of disrepair; a girl stands in the doorway of no.21, and no. 25 is derelict. Both properties were demolished soon after.

GRANGE VALE
SEWER
SECTION 2
14.6.04

9 These road works, looking down Hind Street in 1904, were for the Grange Vale sewer. This was an on-going problem originating when the stream, which ran down what is now Borough Road, was redirected. All the buildings in this picture have been demolished, the most recent being the Wesleyan chapel on the left, which had opened in 1873.

10 This is a continuation of the Grange Vale sewer scheme seen in the previous picture. There had been particular problems here as this is the area where the old stream entered the river Mersey. This low railway bridge in Chester Street had always been a problem with double-decker tramcars, with the top deck being specially converted to cope with the low headroom. The bridge was demolished *c*.1967.

11 Harding's char-a-banc is parked outside the *Britannia Hotel* in Old Chester Road, with Green Lane in the background. The men, who are wood-working machinists from Cammell Laird's shipyard, are waiting to be taken on their annual picnic in 1919. The old firm of Alfred Harding, which was established in 1890, is still operating today from premises in Grange Road West (*see* plate 97).

12 The royal car carrying King George V and Queen Mary is seen approaching the main Green Lane entrance of Cammell Laird in New Chester Road at approximately 3.56 p.m. on Wednesday 25 March 1914. They were greeted by the Chairman, Mr. W.L. Hitchens and the Managing Director, Mr. G.J. Carter, who then escorted them through the shipyard, leaving by the Abbey Street Gate and arriving at the town hall at about 4.35 p.m.

13   This unusual side view of a launch at Cammell Laird was of the *Melbourne,* a 5,400-ton cruiser, taken on 30 May 1912. This ship, which had been built for the Australian Navy, was 456-ft. long and carried a crew of 400 officers and men. All viewing places have been taken up by the large crowd, some of them even standing in the water!

14   Vast crowds have turned out to see the launch at Cammell Laird of the battleship *Prince of Wales* on 3 April 1939. She took part in the sinking of the *Bismark* but she will be best remembered for her rôle in hosting the signing by Winston Churchill and President Roosevelt of the Atlantic Charter. She was torpedoed by aircraft and sunk off Malaysia on 10 December 1941.

15 The Cunard White Star liner *Mauretania* is viewed from afar by four enthusiasts. When she was launched on 28 July 1938, it was said to be the greatest day in the history of Cammell Laird. At 34,000 tons, she was then the largest ship ever built in an English shipyard. She survived the Second World War, even though she carried some 335,000 troops, travelling over half-a-million miles. She was scrapped in 1965.

16 The third ship to be named *Ark Royal* is viewed on the Mersey from the top of a Birkenhead ferry. She was launched at Cammell Laird on 13 April 1937 and was the first ship to be designed and built as an aircraft carrier. She was fitted out prior to the outbreak of war on 3 September 1939, taking part in tracking the *Graf Spee,* and was involved in the sinking of the *Bismark*. She was torpedoed on 13 November 1941 and sank off Gibraltar.

17   The Birkenhead Commissioners leased the Woodside ferry in 1842 and purchased it outright in 1858. The original stone jetty at Woodside was replaced in 1862 with this floating landing stage pictured *c.*1910. In 1863 the first saloon passenger steamship, the *Cheshire*, came into service, followed two years later by the *Lancashire* and *Woodside*. The buildings with the curved roofs, seen in the background, are part of Woodside station.

18   Following the building of the new floating landing stage in 1862, a floating roadway was constructed here in 1868. This enabled horse-drawn vehicles to gain access to and from the landing stage. Initially converted ferry boats were used until the first purpose-built luggage boat, the *Oxton*, came into service in 1879. The luggage boat *Tranmere*, pictured here, was in service from 1884 to 1925.

19 This photograph was used on a Birkenhead Corporation Ferries official postcard which was posted in 1905. It shows a car crossing a Woodside passenger steamer's gangway from the boat onto the floating roadway at Woodside. Motor cars using the passenger steamers were not to exceed 6ft. 3in. in height and 6ft. 5in. in width. This traffic must have been a novelty then, as there were so few cars produced.

20 The luggage boat *Barnston* is approaching the floating landing stage at Woodside in 1933. It is laden with transport and several vehicles are already waiting to be carried across to Liverpool. The service was then at its peak, and could not cope with the demand, but when the Mersey Tunnel opened in 1934 it carried mainly horse-drawn vehicles and petrol tankers, which were not allowed in the tunnel. The service closed in 1939.

WOODSIDE STAGE, BIRKENHEAD.

21 This is a rear view of the other end of the floating landing stage at Woodside, from the previous picture. The ferries were originally the only method of crossing the Mersey to Liverpool. However, competition from the Mersey Railway (opened in 1886), the Mersey Road Tunnel (opened in 1934) and more recently the bus services direct to Liverpool from all parts of Wirral, has led to a decline in passengers using the ferries.

22 This Mersey Ferry Boat *Claughton*, which was acquired in 1930, and the *Bidston,* in 1933, shown in the previous picture, were both built at Cammell Laird. To combat the decline in passenger numbers, the buildings, covered gangway and floating landing stage have all recently been replaced or renovated and the ferry service has now become more of a tourist attraction.

F.S. "CLAUGHTON".

23 The One O'clock Gun, which was situated at Morpeth Pier, is seen facing the river Mersey in the 1920s. Originally sited in Liverpool, it was moved here and was first fired, electrically, from Bidston Observatory on 21 September 1867. It provided a time signal for the shipping trade. Many guns have been used over the years, with the last one firing for the final time on 20 July 1969.

24 This is the aftermath of the Birkenhead Dock disaster on 6 March 1909. A high spring tide, combined with strong winds, caused a coffer dam to collapse, killing 14 workmen who were excavating for the Victoria Dock. The men, who were working 40ft. below the surface, had just changed shift and Tommy Devine, a young man, was the only one snatched to safety.

4·BRIDGES.—
THE FIRST FROM
BIRKENHEAD.

25 Foot passengers can be seen crossing the nearest to Birkenhead of the four bridges between Wallasey and Birkenhead in the 1920s; vehicles are using the roadway behind. This hydraulically-operated swing bridge, which is seen from the East Float looking towards Egerton Dock, was installed about 1866. It was replaced in 1932, as were two other of the bridges, by an electrically operated bascule rolling lift bridge (*see* plate 26).

26 The hydraulic Duke Street swing bridge over the East/West Float passage was photographed in the 1920s, looking towards the East Float. This bridge was opened in 1861, being replaced by the present electrically operated bascule bridge in 1931. Road transport as well as a steam railway engine can be seen crossing the bridge in front of Hall Line's transit shed. Vernon's flour mills can be seen on the extreme right.

DUKE STREET BRIDGE. BIRKENHEAD.

27 Woodside was the terminus for the horse-drawn trams from 1860; however, the track had to be altered when the service was electrified in 1901. Due to the low bridge in Chester Street on the New Ferry route, 13 single-deck trams were purchased, of which two can be seen in the distance. By 1910 they had all been fitted with an upper-deck, lower than normal to allow for the bridge (*see* plate 10).

28 The three men are walking towards the Woodside ferry terminus buildings, *c.*1910. A lady is seen alighting from a New Ferry tram on the left, which was originally one of the single-decker tramcars mentioned in the previous picture and is seen here with a low upper-deck fitted. Although the destination board on this tram states 'Port Sunlight', the terminus was at New Ferry. Woodside station is seen to the right of the picture.

29 Tramcar No.31 is pictured on 24 September 1903, probably in Conway Street. The poster in the window is advertising a reduction from 3d. to 2d. for a round trip on the Circular route. This tramcar usually operated on the Higher Tranmere route, where, because of the gradient, the Board of Trade refused to allow a top cover to be fitted to cars. However, in 1922 the go-ahead was given and they all received top covers by 1928.

30 One of the main problems for the drivers of the Birkenhead electric trams was that the driver's cab was open to the elements. Although many improvements were made to the fleet of 68 tramcars, it was not until 1921 that No.58 was fitted with a driver's windscreen. The only other cars to be fitted in this way (this work was carried out in 1931) were Nos.18 (seen here at Woodside with the windscreen), 36 and 42.

31 Birkenhead Corporation tramcar No.29 is seen standing at Woodside. This four wheeler was one of 31 cars delivered with open tops. However, by 1914 all these trams had had a top cover fitted except Nos.24-36, which operated on the Tranmere route (*see* plate 29). These cars were fitted with top covers from 1922, the work being carried out at the Laird Street joinery shop.

32 Car No.40, the rear one of the two trams, was delivered in 1901 with an open top. It was one of six tramcars fitted with a short top cover by corporation staff in 1914. The two buses in the picture were a sign of the times, with the end of the tram system not far away. The New Ferry route closed in December 1931, followed by the Higher Tranmere and Prenton routes in 1934, the Docks route in 1935 and finally the Circle route in 1937.

33 The crowd is gathered round illuminated tramcar No.22 with Owen Murphy at the controls and the mayor to the right. This tramcar, which was used to celebrate the Coronation of King George VI in May 1937, is being used two months later on 17 July as the last official Birkenhead tram. For the people of Birkenhead this was a sad day for this was the end of an era which had started back in 1860 with Europe's first public tramway system.

34 All traffic has come to a standstill as the 4th Cheshires are marching up Hamilton Street into Hamilton Square. The 4th Battalion Cheshire Regiment are returning home to their headquarters in Grange Road West after their summer camp in 1909. At this time their Honorary Colonel was Colonel F.W. Blood. Everyone in the picture is wearing a hat—the ladies bonnets and the men boaters or flat caps.

35 This Birkenhead School rugby team is seen posing in Hamilton Square Gardens. The unusual feature of this picture is that John Laird's statue, erected in 1877, can be seen behind the boy on the left but the town hall is not yet built. This dates the photograph to between 1877 and 1883, when work started on the town hall. Two of the boys standing are wearing rugby caps they have been awarded.

36 Birkenhead Town Hall, pictured *c*.1900, opened in Hamilton Square in 1887. Built of Storeton stone, this building replaced the original town hall in Hamilton Street. The children on the right are ready to play lawn tennis on the private gardens in the centre of the square. The council purchased these gardens in 1903 and opened them to the public.

37 The town hall, which is bedecked in flags for the 1911 Coronation, is flanked either side by some of the buildings which surround Hamilton Square. The first of these buildings was started in 1826, with the last being completed by the 1850s. The town hall was damaged by fire in 1901 and the tower seen in the previous picture was replaced by the one seen here at a cost of £1,500. Total cost of repairs was £15,000.

38 These men form part of the 1927 Cenotaph parade in Hamilton Square. The Cenotaph, which faces the town hall, was unveiled in 1925 as a memorial to the 1,293 men of Birkenhead who died in the First World War. This replaced the statue of John Laird which had been erected here in 1877. Amid much controversy it was moved to the other side of the square and Birkenhead's first M.P. now has his back to the town hall.

39 The marching band is passing Murphie's Seamen's Outfitters shop at 43 Hamilton Street. The building below the town hall clock is 51-52 Hamilton Square, on the corner of Duncan Street, where Smith & Sons Estate Agents, valuers and property auctioneers, have their offices. The firm, which was founded in 1840, is probably one of Birkenhead's oldest businesses still operating.

40 *(left)* Holy Trinity Anglican Church, seen in Price Street *c.*1910, was opened in 1840. The church came to prominence in the Garibaldi riots of 1862 following a debate of a British parliamentary debating society in the church school. Fighting broke out in a large crowd which held differing political and religious views. The police were called at 7.30p.m. but, due to the numbers involved, they were unable to control the crowd until midnight (*see* plate 42).

41 *(below)* When Holy Trinity Church, was opened in 1840, a school was also opened behind the church, backing onto Brook Street. Initially 120 boys, 130 girls and 90 infants were educated here. The school was enlarged in 1898, which almost doubled the number that could be taught there. This is a boys' class photograph taken at Holy Trinity school in 1927.

42 *(top right)* The *Arab Arms Hotel* is pictured in 1910 on the corner of Watson Street and Brook Street, when John R. Robson was the victualler. This Birkenhead Brewery pub, which dates back to at least 1850, was one of many properties damaged in the riots of 1862. Most of their windows were broken, doors smashed and premises looted following trouble that had originated from Holy Trinity Church in Price Street.

43 *(bottom right)* St Laurence's Roman Catholic church is pictured in Beckwith Street prior to 1910. The original church was opened here in 1866, but due to increasing population a new church was opened in 1874. Disaster befell in 1886 when the church was damaged during the construction of the Mersey Railway and was replaced in 1890. The church continued to serve the area but due to a dwindling population closed in March 1995.

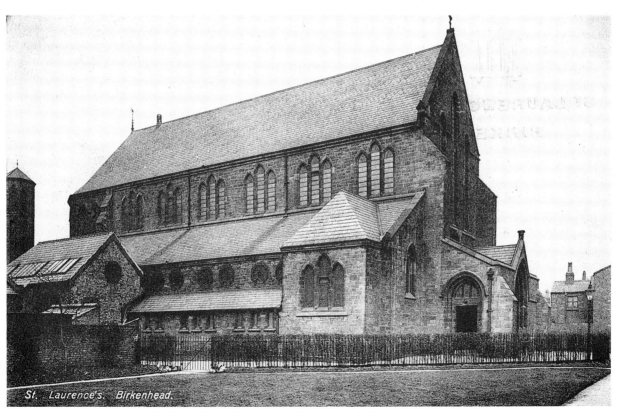

St. Laurence's. Birkenhead.

44 The Birkenhead Brewery Co. Ltd. was registered on 29 August 1865, being formed out of two family breweries, the Cook's in Oxton Road and the Aspinall's in Livingstone Street. This site in Livingstone Street was chosen as there was a well which could supply the brewery's needs. The building, seen here on the corner of Brook Street, which had a date-stone of 1876, was demolished in the 1960s and the site became a garage for the brewery vehicles.

45 Birkenhead Brewery's stables in Northampton Street, Liverpool were photographed *c.*1900 by R.M. Morris of Birkenhead, who also took the previous picture. The brewery's pubs in the Liverpool area were serviced from here, with the Birkenhead depot able to supply their Cheshire and North Wales public houses. The brewery merged with Threlfall's Chester Ltd. in 1962 and was then taken over by Whitbread's Brewery in 1967.

46 These barefoot children are posing on the steps of the Charles Thompson Mission in Hemingford Street, *c*.1910. Charles Thompson moved from Hanley, in the Potteries, to Birkenhead for health reasons, working in a grocery shop for 20 years, then opening a shop of his own. However, he realised his vocation was helping the poor so he opened a meeting room which kept changing location until finally established in premises in Hemingford Street in 1892 (*see* plate 47), where it is situated today.

47 The children attending the Charles Thompson Mission are seen inside the Mission Hall with Father Christmas, the Mayor and Annie Thompson, Charles Thompson's daughter. It was she that took over as Superintendent when he died in 1903. She was awarded the M.B.E. in 1953 and, three years after she died in 1965, the mission was incorporated into the Liverpool City Mission. The good work continues today under Pastor Rob Jeffs.

48 The highlights of the year for the poor children who attended Charles Thompson's Mission were the outings to the country and seaside and the annual camp. The band can be seen leading from the Mission the children who have just arrived by boat at New Brighton. Another popular venue was the camp at Dwygyfylchi, North Wales (this camp was also used by the Shaftesbury Boys' Club—*see* plate 49). The camp closed in 1984.

49 Shaftesbury Street Boys' Club, now known as the Shaftesbury Boys' Club, was founded in 1886. Originally they occupied the Chester Street Mission school and then in 1903 they purchased the Jackson Street Baptist chapel, which was extended to Thomas Street in 1911. Their final move was in 1971 when they moved to Mendip Road. This is a view of their camp kitchen at Dwygyfylchi, North Wales in July 1911.

33

50 Looking up Conway Street towards Argyle Street in 1912 the shops from the left are: Woolman's Printers & Stationers; J.A. Oxton, Clothier & Outfitter; a Merchant Tailor's shop and Black & Sons, Furniture Dealers. Charles Stanley's Confectioners shop at 87, Argyle Street is to the right of the tram pole. The site of the shops pictured in Argyle Street now forms part of the approach roads to the Mersey Tunnel.

51 The policeman on the right is directing traffic from the junction of Argyle Street, looking down Conway Street, *c.*1916. Tramcar No.53, which is approaching the policeman, was built in 1902 as an open top bogie and fitted with a 'White' full-length top-cover by 1905. The tall building to the right of the tram dates back to at least the 1870s when it was the shop and works of Pryce & Delaney, Cabinet Makers and is here a garage.

CONWAY STREET, BIRKENHEAD.   B.H.1

52 The garage seen in the previous picture opened as a cinema in May 1917 and here in the early 1930s is the Empire Picture House. The tram just visible behind Williamson's Baker's cart is on the Oxton Circle route and to the left is the *Conway Arms* on the corner of Claughton Road. This Cain's pub, known as the 'flat iron', was demolished in the 1960s when the area was cleared for the tunnel flyover approach roads and the site is now a car park.

53 This was taken a few years after the picture above. The trams have gone, replaced by buses, and the Empire Cinema on the right has been modernised. This was to be Birkenhead's last cinema, which closed in January 1991. The Super Cinema, the light coloured building by the car, was originally the post office. It was here on 9 September 1900 that George Fell, the night watchman, was brutally murdered. His murderer was never found.

CONWAY STREET, BIRKENHEAD.   B.H.2

54 'Star' Yacht Manufacturers, whose model boats sold world-wide, was founded by Franz Denye in 1922. For centuries his family had built wooden fishing boats near Ostend, Belgium, but after the outbreak of the First World War he decided to escape to England. He eventually settled in Birkenhead, where he founded the family business in Marion Street. This lasted for three generations, closing when the council made a compulsory purchase order in 1990. This group, which is pictured outside the works, includes Peter Denye on the left.

55 *The Old Post Office Hotel* is seen at 95-97, Argyle Street *c*.1910, when H. Freeman was the landlord. The hotel dates back to at least 1860 when Owen Williams was the victualler and it was then called the *Post Office Hotel.* Situated between Conway Street and Oliver Street, the building pictured is still there today but the front has been altered and in recent years it has been licensed under different names.

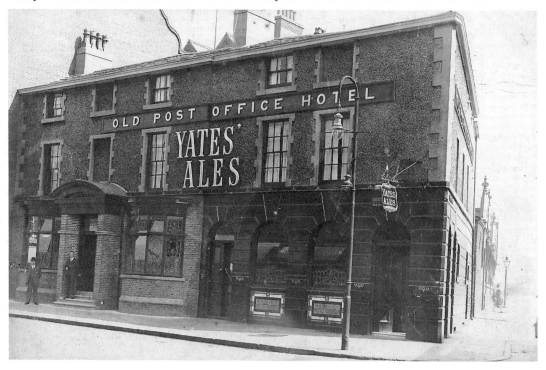

56 Knowles & Jones General Drapers and Silk Mercers store at 4-8 Conway Street is bedecked with flags for the 1911 Coronation. The business, which dated back to the 1870s, flourished until it closed between the wars, with George Sturla & Son later trading here. *The Chester Arms*, a Birkenhead Brewery pub seen on the right, dates back to the 1850s. The building was demolished in 1971 and replaced by St Mark's House office block.

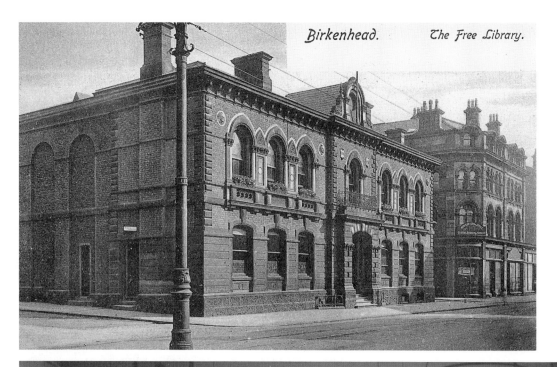

Birkenhead. *The Free Library.*

INTERIOR MUSEUM - ART GALLERY.

57 *(top left)* Birkenhead's first library opened in a shop in Price Street in 1856 but proved so popular it moved to larger premises above the post office in Conway Street (*see* plate 53). In 1864 the first purpose-built free library opened in Hamilton Street, seen here between Library Street and Ewart Street in 1904. This served the town until 1909 when a new central library was opened in Market Place South (*see* plate 59).

58 *(bottom left)* This is an interior view of the Birkenhead Museum and Art Gallery in Hamilton Street. It was established here in 1912, taking over the building vacated by the library which had moved to new premises in Market Place South in 1909. The museum moved to the new purpose-built building in Slatey Road in 1928 (*see* plate 128).

59 *(above)* The new central library is seen in Market Place South, *c.*1910. It was presented to the town by Andrew Carnegie, opened in 1909, and replaced the building in Hamilton Street. However, this new building was doomed, being demolished in 1929 to make way for the Mersey Tunnel entrance. The library moved back into the old Hamilton Street building until the new library was opened in Borough Road in 1934 (*see* plate 78).

BOROUGH OF BIRKENHEAD.

"THE MERSEY TUNNEL BILL, 1925."

POLL OF ELECTORS—Friday, 8th May, 1925,

FROM **8** A.M. TO **8** P.M.

Name of Elector ...*Grillett WR*..

Your No. is...*9667*...........   *Polling District* No. **1 (A) ARGYLE WARD.**

YOUR POLLING STATION IS AT THE

Pilgrim Street Council School.

Application for a Voting Paper should be made to the Presiding Officer at the Polling Station, and you should hand him this card.

If you wish to vote in favour of the promotion of the Bill, you must place a cross (thus **X**) in the column of the Voting Paper headed "FOR." If you wish to vote against the promotion of the Bill, you must place a cross (**X**) in the column headed "AGAINST."

No other mark or writing than a **X** should be placed on the Voting Paper.

VOTE EARLY.   **MARY MERCER,** *Returning Officer.*

Printed and Published by Osborne & Nash, 36 Hamilton Street, Birkenhead.

60 *(top left)* This is an advice card for a poll of the ratepayers of the Borough of Birkenhead on 'The Mersey Tunnel Bill, 1925'. The ratepayers of Liverpool and Bootle also voted on the bill. This referendum in Birkenhead went in favour of connecting Birkenhead and Liverpool by a road tunnel under the River Mersey by a majority of four to one. Work commenced on both sides of the river in December 1925.

62 *(above)* Work on the Queensway Tunnel above ground involved demolishing several buildings, including the Carnegie Free Library and a school. The King Edward VII Memorial Clock had to be resited (*see* plate 74); as many businesses and people were relocated. After eight years of hard work the day finally arrived, 18 July 1934, thousands of spectators cheered the arrival of King George V and Queen Mary at the Birkenhead entrance.

61 *(bottom left)* The boys in the foreground are viewing the work being carried out at what was to be the main entrance to the Queensway Mersey Tunnel. After 27 months of tunnelling, the two groups of workmen met in the middle and the two respective mayors shook hands. There was still much work to be done underground— the tunnel to be enlarged, roadways to be laid and a ventilation system to be constructed. Additionally drainage and lighting had to be provided.

63 This photograph, taken by McUlloch of Rock Ferry, shows some of the residents of a tenement block near the Birkenhead Priory standing behind a pavement picture. This street painting was one of many in the borough to celebrate the opening of the Queensway Mersey Tunnel and was followed by a street party. This and other buildings in surrounding streets were demolished in the 1960s, making way for new approach roads to the tunnel.

64 This is a 1940s view of the Queensway Mersey Tunnel entrance in Birkenhead. In the first year three million vehicles used the tunnel and by 1959 this number had risen to 11 million. It was decided that a new two-lane tunnel would be the answer. A pilot tunnel was completed in 1967 and work began in 1968, by which time 17 million vehicles were using the Queensway tunnel. The new Kingsway Mersey Tunnel from Wallasey to Liverpool opened on 2 June 1971.

65 The long premises on the left in the previous picture is Birkenhead Market. The Fruit & Vegetable part of the market is seen prior to 1909, when the building pictured on the left was extended and then provided covered accommodation. This market building, which had been erected in 1845 and replaced the original 1835 one, was partly destroyed by fire in 1974.

66 This interior photograph of Birkenhead Market was taken prior to the First World War. Over the years, several suicide attempts took place by jumping from the steel-structured roof; many were successful. By 1950 there were 44 shops against the inner walls and 120 stalls in the body of the building. The market was partly destroyed by fire in 1974, and moved to its present site in 1977.

67 The Argyle Theatre, pictured on the left in Argyle Street, was opened on 21 December 1868 by Dennis Grannell, proprietor of the Rotunda Music Hall, Liverpool. In 1876 the theatre was improved, the name changed to the Prince of Wales Theatre and plays were presented here. It was Mr. Grannell's nephew, Dennis Clarke, who took the theatre to its greatest success after he became sole manager in 1891.

68 *(below)* One of Dennis Clarke's first decisions as manager of the theatre was to restore the name 'Argyle' and bring back the more popular music hall programmes. This move was a great success as he brought all the top stars here and broke all previous receipt records. Vesta Tilley, pictured in one of her costumes, was one of the leading variety hall artistes who entertained the Birkenhead audiences.

69 *(left)* Harry Lauder made his first appearance at this theatre as an unknown 'Irish' Comedian in the 1890s for a fee of £4. He had used up all his successful Irish material in the first half. However, he turned to his Scottish comedian act in the second half and proved to be even more popular with the audience. So a star was born and Dennis Clarke immediately offered him a long contract which resulted in his return to the Argyle many times.

70 *(top right)* The poster on the left, dated 8 March 1897, shows that Vesta Tilley was definitely 'top of the bill' prior to making her third tour through America. The Harry Lauder poster, dated 5 December 1904, also advertises The Bioscope (moving pictures). The Argyle claimed to be the first theatre outside London to show animated pictures, running electric cables through Birkenhead, in 1896, to the theatre where the films were projected onto a sheet.

71 *(right)* This 1930s cartoon postcard is advertising radio broadcasts from the Argyle. This theatre became the first music hall to broadcast live on the radio when Leslie Strange went on the air 14 April 1931. Following this successful broadcast, the theatre arranged for a series of relays from the Argyle to National and Commonwealth programmes. They were also the first theatre to broadcast direct to the U.S.A.

72 *(far right)* Over the years, many other famous stars have appeared on the stage of the Argyle including Charlie Chaplin, W.C. Fields, G.H. Elliot, George Formby (who made his stage debut here), Stan Laurel and Donald Peers (pictured here). It was at the Argyle that Flanagan & Allen first performed 'Underneath the Arches'. The theatre received a direct hit on 21 September 1940 and was destroyed. Part of Beatties' car park occupies the site today.

DON'T TINKER ABOUT! Have YOUR set adjusted by an expert in time for the the next Broadcast from the ARGYLE, Birkenhead, on

73 The children pictured in 1914 are probably pupils of St Paul's Church schools seen on the left. The houses on the right in Borough Road, many of which were theatrical lodgings, were demolished in the 1960s to make way for the new approach roads for the Mersey Tunnel. The King Edward VII Memorial Clock Tower, which was unveiled in Argyle Street in 1912 was moved *c.*1929 (*see* plate 74).

74 The clock tower was moved to this site between Borough Road and Clifton Crescent *c.*1929 from nearer Central station, due to the New Mersey Tunnel Approach Road Scheme. The *Central Hotel*, pictured on the left, was built by local builders Lloyd & Cross in 1938. Today the area is dominated by the flyover for one of the Mersey Tunnel approach roads.

75 Birkenhead Central station, pictured here, and Hamilton Square station, were the two intermediate stations on the Mersey Line which opened on 20 January 1886 and ran between Green Lane, Tranmere and Liverpool James Street. Conditions for the traveller on the steam trains were poor due to the smoke-filled tunnel, but the journey improved when the line was electrified in May 1903.

MAY DAY PROCESSION. BIRKENHEAD. 12/5/06. No 2.

76 *(top left)* This photograph of the May Day procession on 12 May 1906 was taken from Central station buildings. The firemen on the right-hand float are passing in front of the Argyle Street South Public Baths. Opening in 1882, they contained vapour baths, a slipper and shower bath as well as the swimming pool. The baths were demolished and a garage now occupies the site.

77 *(left)* Looking down Argyle Street South *c.*1938, where this steep hill had posed a problem for the engineers working on the Higher Tranmere tramway route at the turn of the century. The difficulty of the 1 in 7 gradient was overcome by constructing Pearson Road, seen on the right, which reduced the gradient to 1 in 13.5. The tram lines can still be seen here although by this time the trams had ceased operating and buses taken over.

78 *(above)* Following the demolition of the library in Market Place South, to make way for the Mersey Tunnel entrance, this new purpose-built library was erected in Borough Road. The royal car is seen parked outside the new building with King George V about to open it officially by pressing a switch which parted the Union Jack flags over the entrance; the doors then automatically opened.

79 This row of shops is in Borough Road in 1910, between Harrowby Road on the right and Elmswood Road. Melling's chemist and optician shop on the right also advertises a public telephone; next door is J. Threadgold, fruiterer and poultry; then a branch of John Irwin & Sons, grocer, whose hand-cart can be seen outside the shop; A. Smith, family butcher and J.G. Lea, confectioner. Note the tram lines and setts.

80 The road repairs are taking place outside the Borough Motor Works in Borough Road at its junction with Kingsland Road. The business was established here *c*.1912 by two brothers, John and Edward Johnston, who were taxi cab proprietors. In 1915 they advertised 'A day and night service with up-to-date cars, open or closed, any distance day or night'. The business was sold *c*.1956 to a petrol company and until recently a petrol station operated here.

81 The Royal car is proceeding along Borough Road to Rock Ferry station after King George V had opened the Mersey Tunnel and the new Central Library on 18 July 1934. The car is passing Borough Motor Works, seen in the previous picture, and to the right is the Kingsland dance hall and Plaza cinema. Large crowds can be seen lining the road, with all the buildings bedecked with bunting.

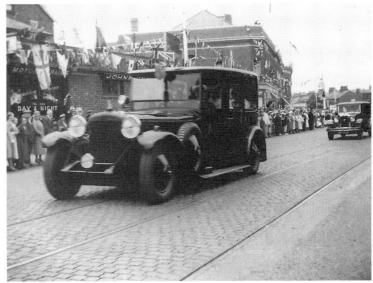

82 The Johnston Brothers who set up the Borough Motor Works, seen in the previous two pictures, also operated a bus service to Heswall. The Daimler 20-seater seen here was bought in August 1922 and the other vehicle they used was a 32-seater Leyland char-a-banc. The service to Heswall was sold to Alfred Harding of Charing Cross (*see* plate 97) on 1 October 1924, who then sold it to Crosville Motor Co. in October 1925.

TRANMERE ROVERS. F. C. (SEASON 1907-8)

W. Hardie. R. Jones. A. McAfee. R. Macdonald.
J. Thomas. A. Hilton. D. Muir. J. Lee. H. Viner. W. Ingram. F. Milner. E. Thomas. [Trainer] E. Prince. R. Ledsome.
[Ass. Trainer]   T. Hill. H. Buck. Franklin. H. Fishwick. E. Jones. T. Butler.

83   This Tranmere Rovers F.C. team of 1907-8 were champions of the Combination. However, the club resigned from this league in 1909 and joined the Lancashire Combination. The club had been founded as Belmont in 1884, changing its name to Tranmere Rovers in 1885. They moved to their present Borough Road ground in 1912. The previous 25 years were spent on a ground in Temple Road, which is now the site of Devonshire Park school.

84   This view of the crowd on the Spion Kop at Tranmere Rovers' ground, Prenton Park, was taken on 30 March 1923 when the opposition was Wigan Borough in the Football League Division Three North. Both Rovers and Wigan Borough were founder members of this league in the 1921/2 season. It was in 1921 that the 11-acre site at Prenton Park was purchased for £7,500, which was to prove an excellent decision in future years.

GOOD FRIDAY AT PRENTON   A VIEW OF SPION KOP
ROVERS V WIGAN BOROUGH

ROYAL ENGINEERS
AT WORK BRIDGE BUILDING

No 7

85 The Royal Engineers are busy bridge-building across a pond on land adjacent to Tranmere Rovers' football ground, seen on the left, in 1915. The hedge behind the soldiers is in Borough Road and the water tower on the horizon is in Tower Road, Higher Tranmere, but is no longer there today. The message on this postcard from one of the soldiers said that they were shortly leaving for the Dardanelles.

86 *(left)* This 1930s view of Mount Road was taken from Borough Road. The shops then were from the left: Miss L. Jones—confectioner; National Provincial Bank; Garden Stores; empty; Charles H. Prince—tobacconist; Mount Chandlery Stores; Lunts—bakers; Constance Miller—drapers; Walter Cowie—chemist and Branch No.57 of the Birkenhead & District Co-operative Society.

87 *(below left)* The people of Tranmere posing here are probably some of those who have helped to build this 20-ft. high bonfire in Mersey Park. The occasion was the Coronation of George V on 22 June 1911, when, as well as the bonfire, there were two firework displays in the area, one here and one in Birkenhead Park. Mersey Park, with 21 acres of land, was opened to the public on 25 July 1885 and had a fine outlook over the river Mersey.

88 *(below)* St Luke's Church is seen on the right in Old Chester Road in 1909. The church, which was built in 1881 of red sandstone, had 653 sittings and was formed on 6 March 1883 as a consolidated chapelry out of St Catherine and St Paul, Tranmere. St Luke's School, seen beyond Mersey Mount (the road on the left) was opened in 1884, closed down in the 1960s and, after St Luke's Church, the demolition of the levelled site now forms part of Mersey Park.

89 Arudy, a continental-style chateau, was built in the 1860s by Victor Poutz in what was then Bebington 'Lane', later changed to Bebington Road. By 1904, it had become The Towers. It was subsequently purchased by Birkenhead Corporation and incorporated into Victoria Park, which had been opened to the public in 1901. During the First World War it was used for Belgian refugees and was later converted into flats by the Corporation. It was demolished *c*.1965.

90 The Gladstone Liberal club, which opened *c*.1900, is seen on the immediate left in Church Road, Higher Tranmere *c*.1910. Further down on the same side, the No.29 tramcar is passing Walker Street, with the *Bee Hive* public house on the far corner dating back to at least 1879, when the victualler was John Garnham. The row of shops on the right were demolished in the 1970s and the road widened. St Catherine's Church is seen in the distance.

91 This group of Birkenhead Corporation tramway drivers, conductors and inspector are posing between tram Nos.30 and 26 in Church Road, Tranmere in 1914. They are about to transport the aged, blind and infirm from the Tranmere Institution to the Charles Thompson Mission rooms in Hemingford Street for their annual treat. The three tramcars used were supplied free of charge by the Birkenhead Corporation Tramways Department.

92 This is a different view of the trams, with the building in the previous picture forming part of the former Tranmere Workhouse, being built 1862-3. The development from workhouse into hospital took shape from the turn of the century. New buildings were erected on the Elm Road side of the site and in 1911 the hospital and workhouse were separated, the hospital taking over the whole of the premises *c.*1930. During both World Wars, the wounded were treated here and by 1948, there were more than 800 beds. St Catherine's Hospital today specialises in the elderly and psychiatric patients.

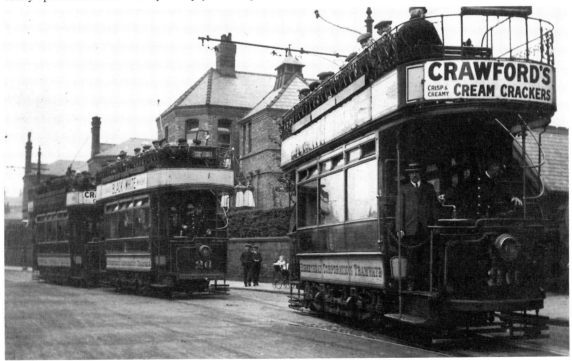

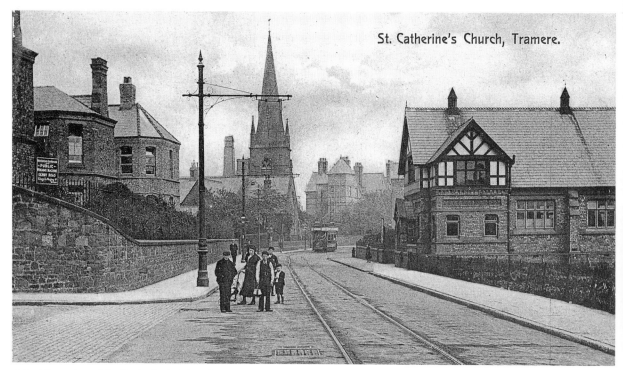

St. Catherine's Church, Tramere.

93 The spire of St Catherine's Church, Tranmere, can be seen in the distance in Church Road on this postcard that was sent in 1912. The brick church of 1831 was altered and enlarged in 1875-6 when there were 800 sittings, with the tower and spire being added in 1879. St Catherine's Church Institute, which is seen on the right, was erected in 1892 at a cost of £2,300 with two halls, one seating 500 and the other 120.

94 This early 19th-century building, which stood at the top of Whetstone Lane, was once a private residence with commanding views across the Mersey. It was purchased in 1856 by the Faithful Companions of Jesus and opened as the girl's boarding school Holt Hill Convent, having moved from Hamilton Square. In 1886 a small day school opened here but it was not until 1903 that the two schools were amalgamated. This is a front view of the convent in the early part of this century.

95 By 1910 Holt Hill Convent, seen in the previous picture, had nuns looking after 50 boarders and 100 day pupils. In 1932 the boarding school closed and by 1944, when there were 500 pupils, the convent was recognised as a Direct Grant Grammar school. The physics laboratory, pictured in 1912, had changed little 50 years on. The school moved to Noctorum High in 1981 and the buildings were demolished the following year.

96 The tramcar in the centre of this 1906 picture is in Whetstone Lane on the Charing Cross line, a temporary route which operated from 1903-6, due to sewer works in Borough Road. The shop on the left is Charing Cross Cycle & Motor Works, beyond them is R.J. Reed, window blind manufacturer and the tall building is the Birkenhead fire station. This opened in 1895 and operated here until it moved to its present site in Exmouth Street in 1973.

97 Alfred Harding's horse-drawn removal vehicle, which is pictured *c.*1900, advertises 'Estimates Free to Families Removing and Storing'. By 1915, the firm, which was originally based in Rock Ferry, had moved to premises in Charing Cross. They advertised that furniture could be loaded and delivered 100 miles away on the same day.

98 Besides being a Removal & Storage Contractor, as seen in the previous picture, by 1915 Alfred Harding had also become a Motor Char-a-banc Operator. This AEC vehicle was not all it seemed, for at their Charing Cross depot a removable top could be lowered by hoist onto the char-a-banc and convert it into a removal van. The company still operates from Grange Road West today.

99 The Unitarian chapel is pictured in Charing Cross in the 1890s. The chapel, which was erected in 1851 at a cost of £1,600, was built in the gothic style and had 320 sittings. The site had become a valuable asset by the turn of the century and was sold, to be replaced by Bank Building (*see* plate 100). The church was resited in Bessborough Road.

100 The parade of sea scouts has just marched up Grange Road and into Charing Cross. Behind the crowds and in the background is Exmouth Street with Bank Building to the left, which replaced the church seen in the previous

picture, opening in 1901. This is the only building in the picture still standing today. The *Grange Hotel*, photographed on the right, can be seen in the next picture.

GRANGE ROAD

BIRKENHEAD, 104

101 *(above)* Grange Road is behind the policeman who is standing under the lamp post. The Birkenhead Brewery pub on the left, the *Grange Hotel* (*see* plate 100), was demolished in the 1980s and the site is now a fast food restaurant. The North & South Wales Bank building on the right, which was completed in 1902, later became a branch of the Midland Bank and is now a bistro.

102 *(top right)* Grange Road Baptist church, which opened in 1858 and had seating for 600, is pictured in Grange Road at its junction with Catherine Street, to the left. The site was sold to Woolworth's in the 1930s, who built their present store here. With the proceeds the new chapel was built in Whetstone Lane in 1939, but was not completed until after the war. Part of the Y.M.C.A. building can be seen on the right (*see* plate 103).

103 *(bottom right)* Looking down Grange Road in 1913, the doorway on the left was the entrance to the Y.M.C.A., whose carved initials above the door can still be seen today. Opening in November 1890, it operated from here until 1934, when it moved to new premises in Whetstone Lane. This building will be remembered as the venue for Lord Baden-Powell's inaugural meeting of the Boy Scout movement, and it was a proud moment when the borough was asked to host the International Jamboree on the 21st anniversary of its founding here (*see* plate 173).

Birkenhead.
Grange Road Baptist Church.

WILLIAM PYKE

Watchmaker and Jeweller

227 Grange Road, & 42 & 44 Market Street,

BIRKENHEAD.

A Splendid Assortment of Watches, Clocks, Jewellery and Electro Plate.

ENGLISH & FOREIGN WATCHES & CLOCKS REPAIRED BY SKILLED MEN.

CLOCKS WOUND BY CONTRACT.   A TRIAL SOLICITED.

104 Palfryman and Pyke, jewellers and watchmakers, started business at 31 Market Street in 1877. This was then the main shopping and business area in Birkenhead. By 1890, the business had moved to 42-44 Market Street and they had opened a branch at 227 Grange Road. This 1892 advert shows that William Pyke had become the sole proprietor. The following year they relocated to their present and main premises at 237 Grange Road.

105 Hancock's Pianos and Organs sign is seen above the shop at 215-219 Grange Road at its junction with Horatio Street. However, the shop on the ground floor is occupied by Timpson's Shoes and advertises 'Sockless Boots' at 10s. 6d. The building at the far end of this block is St Werburgh's R.C. Junior Boys School which opened in 1850 and remained here over 100 years before moving to Park Close, off Whetstone Lane.

106 The Metropole Theatre, pictured in Grange Road *c.*1906, was opened here in 1888 as Ohmy's Grand Circus. This venture was not successful and within two years it became the Gaiety Music Hall which lasted until 1898 when it became the Metropole Theatre, was famous for its drama productions. In 1908 it was totally renovated, having been closed for three years, and became the Hippodrome Theatre of Varieties. The building was bought by the Birkenhead Co-op in the mid-1930s.

107 The crowds in Grange Road are watching the Children's Day procession in 1926. 'The Voyage of Life' tableau is mounted on a cart loaned by Crutchley, coal merchant. The sign for A. Murphie's pawnbrokers and jewellers shop at 90 Grange Road is seen above Allanson's stores, the single-storied shops at nos. 92-98. This was to become a two-storied building which was later purchased by Beatties (*see* plate 108).

108 Allanson's stores, seen in the previous picture and photographed here *c.*1950, dates back to 1860. It was then that John Allanson and his sister opened a small draper's shop on part of this site. In 1934 the business became a public company with considerable reconstruction and extension work being carried out. On 29 September 1940 the store was badly damaged by incendiaries, but soon reopened. In 1964, the firm sold out to Beatties.

109 St Werburgh's Roman Catholic Church, which is seen on the left, is situated at the bottom of Grange Road, having been opened on 15 August 1837. In 1941, the girls and infants school in adjoining Austin Street, which were affiliated to the church, were destroyed by bombing and at the same time the church was damaged. St Werburgh's, which still flourishes today, is known as 'the shopper's church'.

110 Taken at the same time as plate 101, but looking in the other direction up Grange Road West, the policeman is still on duty under the lamp post. The ornate building on the right was a branch of the Bank of Liverpool and, although no longer a bank, it boasts a stained-glass window which depicts the emblem of the Bank of Liverpool. It was once the site of the Unitarian chapel (*see* plate 99).

111 John Evans, the local agent for the Halifax Building Society, is seen discussing business with a prospective customer. Here he is seen operating from a trade stand although his business premises were the Charing Cross Estate Offices at 10, Oxton Road. He later moved to Hamilton Square and his business was eventually taken over by Smith & Sons, which was founded in 1840 (*see* plate 39).

112 The policeman is standing by the lamp post in the centre of Charing Cross during the First World War. Waiting patiently by his side is Laddie the dog, who is collecting funds on behalf of the Red Cross for the local wounded soldiers. The poster records that £130 had already been raised.

113 Rioting in Birkenhead during the First World War was caused by the sinking of the Cunarder, *Lusitania*, pictured in the Mersey in 1907, by a German submarine. Built in 1904-6, at a cost of £1.3m, she weighed 32,500 tons and was 706ft. long. The ship went down on 7 May 1915 with the loss of 1,198 lives, including many Merseysiders. When news of the tragedy filtered through, many German-sounding businesses were attacked.

114 The Misses Bendix's Milliner and Draper's shop, 41 Woodchurch Road, at the junction of Glover Street, was one of the premises wrecked and looted following the *Lusitania* disaster. Although the crowd was convinced that they were Germans, they had in fact been born in Woolton, Liverpool and had never been out of the country. Many other innocent people had premises vandalised and looted.

115 One of the worst of the *Lusitania* riot attacks, was on Charles Dashley's pork butcher's shop, 35 Oxton Road, on 10 May 1915. Over 20 policemen were unable to hold back the crowd who broke all the windows and threw the contents of the shop and house into the road, setting fire to it. This was the scene the following day, where the shops either side show no signs of damage.

116 Taken from Charing Cross looking up Oxton Road, the Royal Insurance building seen on the right was later to become a branch of the District Bank Limited. This pre-First World War picture shows the cobbled street and only horse-drawn vehicles can be seen. The lady on the left, whose picture is blurred, is passing the *Park Hotel* and, beyond her, the horse and cart is standing outside Robinson's Ironmongers & Gas-fitters shop.

117 T. Lennox's newsagent's shop is pictured at 36 Oxton Road prior to 1910. William Lennox, who is pictured in the doorway, was once a blacksmith in the Lake District. However, as there was little work for him, he became a boilermaker at Barrow-in-Furness. About 1870, he came to Birkenhead, working at Laird's until he retired. It was then he bought this newsagent's shop and lived above, selling it in about 1920.

118 Taken from the upstairs window of 36 Oxton Road, the buildings seen in the distance are in Charing Cross and at the top of Grange Road. The flags to celebrate the 1911 Coronation cross over the road to John Duff's Oxton Road bakery. The building with the two flagpoles is Tutty's stores which operated in Oxton Road from 1904 to 1937, when Rostances took over, trading here until 1977.

119 Looking down Grange Road West prior to the First World War, the road to the right is Westbourne Road and to the left, behind the ornate lamp post, is Eastbourne Road. The horse and cart on the left belong to and are standing outside W. Singleton & Son, Bakers at no.60, and the shop beyond, no.58, on the corner of Eastbourne Road is L. Pollock, bassinette maker (hooded wicker cradle or pram), later to become Pollock's Prams.

120 Founded in Clifton Crescent in 1845 as the 'Birkenhead Ladies Charitable Institution and Lying-in Hospital', it had moved to 108, Conway Street by 1879 and to here in Grange Mount by 1891. This home-from-home hospital changed its name to the Birkenhead Maternity Hospital in 1913 and has been the birthplace of thousands of local children. It closed in 1978, transferring its maternity services to St Catherine's Hospital, Tranmere.

121 John Lewis, family butcher of 79 Westbourne Road (off Grange Road West), can be seen in the shadow of his doorway. His delivery bicycle, with basket in front, is standing outside the shop. Butchers would advertise their meat by hanging the carcasses outside their premises for all to view and admire. Today health inspectors would have something to say if meat were displayed in this manner.

122 Looking up Westbourne Road in 1914, David Evans' chandler's shop at no.89 is seen on the left at the corner of Ridley Street and Wm. Try's confectioner's and fancy dealer's shop at no.92 is opposite. Both these single-storey shops, which were built on to the front of existing houses, have since been demolished. Charles Willmer, founder of the *Birkenhead News* in 1877, once lived in the house whose chimney can be seen on the right.

CONGREGATIONAL CHURCH, OXTON ROAD, BIRKENHEAD.

"The Unique Series"

123 The Oxton Congregational Church is seen at the junction of Woodchurch Road on the left and Balls Road on the right. This site was chosen *c*.1856 and the church, which cost £5,500 to build, opened on 22 June 1858. A further £2,600 was spent in 1888 on the church tower and schoolroom. The church was completely gutted by fire in February 1922, a month after being altered and redecorated. It reopened on 27 September 1923. The pinnacles have since been removed.

124 Looking up Woodchurch Road in the 1890s, the single-storey building on the left is the Hermitage British School and Free Christian Church. This building later housed the Welsh Calvinistic Methodist chapel and more recently the Elim Pentecostal Church. The present occupiers are the Wirral Family Centre. The *Royal Hotel*, pictured on the right beyond the shops, dates back to at least 1879 when Joseph Wright was the victualler.

125 Looking down Woodchurch Road towards Birkenhead, the tower of the Congregational Church (*see* plate 123) can be seen in the background. James Lucas' poulterer's and fishmonger's shop is seen on the left at the junction with Heathfield Road and behind the large tree is the *Royal Hotel*, seen in the previous picture.

126 These boys from Group VI of Woodchurch Road council school are posing in front of the Senior Girls' entrance. The school, which opened here in a temporary iron building in 1901, transferred to the new building on 5 September 1904 and is still operating here today, but now called the Woodchurch Road primary school.

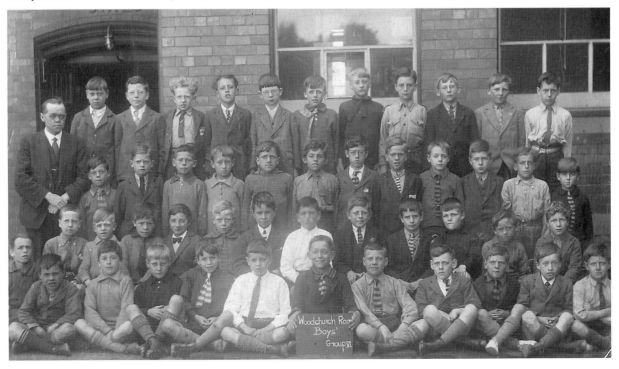

127 The two cars are seen prior to 1910 outside Forde & Wright's Cheshire Motor Works at 14 Balls Road. They were agents for Gladiator cars and had a workshop at 40a Beresford Road. By 1915, the business had become R.E. Wright & Co. who owned another garage at 32a Grange Mount. They had moved from these premises by the mid-1940s and opened a larger garage at 790 Borough Road.

128 John Williamson, a former commissioner for Birkenhead and shipowner, left £20,000 in his will for the erection of a museum and art gallery. This was to be paid on the death of his son. However, his son, Mr. P.A. Williamson, survived his father by only four years and directed that a further £20,000 be added towards his father's bequest. This resulted in the Williamson Art Gallery being opened in Slatey Road on 1 December 1928.

129 Balls Road is pictured in 1906, looking towards Oxton. Barnard Road is on the right beyond the two buildings at nos.62 and 64-68. When the road was widened in 1921, these buildings lost their front gardens. At the same time the single track at this point, on the Oxton-Claughton tram route, was doubled. The houses are still there today but without their charming front gardens.

130 *(top left)* The Birkenhead Pavilion and Roller Skating Rink, which opened at 1a Park Road East on 26 September 1892, could accommodate 1,000 skaters. By 1908 this had become a billiard hall and in 1910 the Claughton Roller Skating Rink opened in Claughton Road on the corner of Cole Street. This was the home of the Claughton Rink hockey team who are posing here in full kit, including roller skates (*see* plate 131).

132 *(above)* Birkenhead Park main entrance is seen from the junction of Park Road East and Park Road North. Above the centre archway, which has an 18-ft. span and is 43-ft. high, are the arms of Birkenhead. Either side of this impressive ionic-style archway is a smaller pedestrian arch, flanked by two-storey lodges.

131 *(bottom left)* The Claughton Roller Skating Rink, which had opened on the site of the headquarters of D Squadron Denbighshire Hussars Imperial Yeomanry, closed down in the 1920s. Cole Street junior mixed and infants school was built on the site, opening in 1929. It is now known as Cole Street primary school. The children of group seven are pictured here soon after the school was opened.

133 The idea of a park in Birkenhead was that of Sir William Jackson who approached Joseph Paxton (later knighted and famous for his design of the Crystal Palace) with the idea of converting 125 acres of marshes into the country's first public park. The work was started in 1844 and took 1,000 men three years to complete. This view, taken in 1907, shows part of the eight acres of lakes, the spoil being made into hillocks within the park.

134 A directory of 1860 describes the park thus: '... was laid out with the most pleasing variety of landscape gardening, adorned with picturesque lakes, flower beds, rockeries, sloping mounds, sculpture, ornamental bridges, serpentine walks and lodges in various styles of architecture, with extensive carriage drives, cricket and archery grounds ...'. On the right is an ornamental building designed as a bandstand-cum-boathouse.

ONLY.

W. JONES, M.G.C. HOBDAY, J.R. DAVIES, J. DAVIDSON, C.M. THOMPSON, W.L. GODFREY, J.B. OLDHAM, R.L. HOLMES
CRAIGMILE, W.M. LOWREY, K.M. LOCKE, R.P. BLOOR, R.J. MARTIN, R.B.V. MAXWELL, F.B. JOHNSTON
CHESHIRE COUNTY RUGBY TEAM 1922

135 The 1922/3 Cheshire rugby team is pictured at Birkenhead Park. The local players worth noting are Craigmile, Lowrey, Locke and Bloor, who were all internationals or trialists and played for Birkenhead Park. 'Charlie' Jones, a Welsh 2nd row, was also a master at Birkenhead School from 1933-58. Birkenhead Park, founded in 1871, moved to this ground in 1886 and a year later hosted its first of three internationals in 1887, 1894 and 1896.

136 Birkenhead School of Art, pictured in Park Road North in 1903, was a gift to the town from John Laird M.P. The building, which opened on 27 September 1871, was then part of Conway Street that was renamed Park Road North in 1891. Due to the rationalisation of education in the 1980s the building was vacated and remained empty until it was restored, reopening as the headquarters of Stanton Marine in 1993.

137 Birkenhead Borough Hospital was another gift to the town from John Laird (*see* plate 136); built at a cost of £5,000 it opened in 1863. Initially it contained three men's wards and one ladies' ward, with accommodation for 50 beds. It was extended several times and in 1926 it changed its name to the Birkenhead General Hospital. The hospital closed when Wirral's hospital services were largely centralised at Arrowe Park Hospital in 1982 and has since been demolished.

138 Williams Brothers' grocery store is pictured at 119 Duke Street, at its junction with Park Road North, in 1913. This was one of the 10 grocery stores owned by Williams Brothers in the Birkenhead area at that time, with the shop today selling fishing tackle. The shop beyond was a sub post office and still is today, with Arthur Hignett's cash draper's next door, now a branch of Hurst's bakery, a Birkenhead firm founded in 1901.

139 St Elizabeth's Convent is pictured in Park Road North in the early part of this century. The Sisters of Charity purchased the property at a reduced price from Mr. Lever and the convent opened on 15 February 1900. The Sisters carried out their work of caring for the sick and poor, instructing converts, assisting the clergy and later working in St Winefride's School. The convent moved to Eleanor Road, Bidston in 1969.

140 *(top left)* The masters are seen on the steps of Birkenhead Proprietary School in Park Road North, *c.*1864. The school was founded here in 1860, opening in the same month as Birkenhead's famous tramway. There were 60 private schools in the area then of which only this one survives today. The school outgrew these premises (which are still there today), moving to new buildings in Shrewsbury Road in 1871 and changing its name to Birkenhead School.

142 *(above)* This 1950 aerial view of the Birkenhead School complex shows Beresford Road to the right and Bidston Road in the foreground. The large building to the left was the 'new schools' building, which was acquired in 1920 and demolished in 1957, making way for the new science block. The junior school building to the right, Overdale, was opened in 1931, having been presented to the school by Graham White M.P., an old boy of the school.

141 *(bottom left)* These Birkenhead Prep. schoolboys are posing in their costumes for the 'Elizabethan Fayre' which was held at the school to celebrate the Coronation of 1953 and to raise funds for the school. The buildings from the left are: the cricket pavilion, opened 1910; the gymnasium, built 1903; the 'big school block' (the first school buildings to be erected on this site, in 1871) and, to the right, the school chapel which opened in 1883.

143 The Oxton Local Board offices, which later housed the police and fire services, were built at 7 Village Road, Oxton, in 1874. Birkenhead High School for Girls was founded here in 1885, moving to Devonshire Place in 1905 (*see* plate 144). The First Church of Christ Scientist operated here from 1925-6, until transferring to Clive Road in 1980. The building was demolished soon afterwards and Village Court flats now occupy the site.

144 The girls' netball court is seen in front of the main entrance to Belgrano, Birkenhead High School, in the early part of this century. They had moved from the building seen in the previous picture, to Devonshire Place in 1905, when there were 40 pupils. The school, which had been taken over by the Girls' Public Day School Company (now Trust) in 1901, expanded, buying surrounding land and property (*see* plate 145).

145 The area inside the white lines belonged to Birkenhead High School when this aerial photograph was taken in the 1930s. The side view of Belgrano, seen in the previous picture, is the house inside the white lines on the right. The buildings opposite the end of Alton Road, seen bottom right at its junction with Devonshire Place, have since been demolished and the swimming pool complex was built on part of the site.

146 This is an artist's impression of St Anselm's College, Manor Hill, which was founded when the Christian Brothers purchased the stone residence Outwood. Building commenced in January 1933 but, due to lack of funds and the outbreak of war, was not completed until 1951, with many additions since. Redcourt, in Devonshire Place was acquired for the preparatory department and in 1954, Oakhurst, an adjoining property in Manor Hill, was bought for the sixth form.

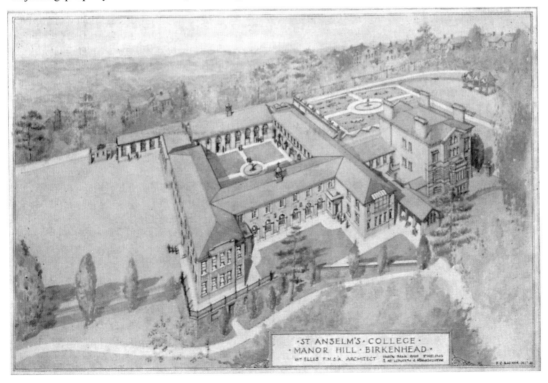

147 This group of tutors, ordinands and principal, Rev. F.B. Heiser, is pictured in front of the dining hall at St Aidan's College in the 1930s. Founded in 1846 by Rev. Joseph Baylee, its aim was to prepare men for the ministry of the Church of England. Standing in six acres of land between Shrewsbury Road and Forest Road, the main building was erected in 1856 at a cost of £40,000. The college was demolished in 1969 and houses were built on the site.

148 Tramcar No. 44 is standing in the Kingsmead Road loop in Shrewsbury Road, which is where trams on this Circle route were timed to meet. This was the last route to close on the Birkenhead tramway on 17 July 1937, prior to handing over to the buses. The sign board to the right of the tram belongs to All Saints' Church (*see* plate 149).

149 The lady with the suitcase, who is probably waiting for a tram, is pictured in front of All Saints' Church, Shrewsbury Road. Built of brick at a cost of £1,500, it was consecrated on All Saints' Day, 1 November 1879. The Parish of All Saints' and St Bede's was formed in January 1911 from St Saviour's Oxton. This church was demolished in the 1970s and flats were built on the site.

150 *(left)* Trinity Presbyterian Church of England is pictured in Beresford Road. When the church was opened on 11 October 1866, the cost of £8,000 seemed an ambitious investment as the church was surrounded then by open fields and few buildings. However, within a few years houses replaced the open fields and in 1892 the new vestry, session and committee rooms were built. In 1977, the church went into partnership with Palm Grove Methodists (*see* plate 151).

151 *(above)* This photograph was taken from Palm Grove in 1905, looking down Lorne Road. Palm Grove Church, seen on the right, was started in 1871 and completed in 1887. The most famous pupil of the Sunday school, which was situated under the chancel, was F.E. Smith, later to become Lord Birkenhead. The church formed a partnership with Trinity Church (*see* plate 150), becoming Trinity with Palm Grove in 1977 and this building was then demolished.

152 *(right)* The entrance to Christ Church, Claughton, is seen in Christchurch Road in 1920. The church, which was built of red sandstone from local Claughton Firs quarry at a cost of £10,000, was opened in February 1849 but not dedicated until May 1854. Underneath the church were large schoolrooms but they were unable to cope with the increasing numbers so in 1883, Claughton Higher Grade School was opened in Borough Road.

153 The Arno was once a quarry supplying red sandstone for local use, but by the turn of the century it had not been used for some time. It was bought by the Corporation in two lots, the last being in 1912 when the six-acre site was opened to the public as a recreational area and included a quoiting pitch, seen on the left. The building to the right is the rear of the National School buildings in Storeton Road and the ivy-clad building is in Mount Olive.

154 The girls are looking out from the Edmond Taylor memorial sun-dial in an elevated position on the Arno. It was Edmond Taylor who played a prominent part in securing the Arno for the public (*see* plate 153). The buildings in the distance are on the far side of Woodchurch Road, with only allotments on this side of the road in this 1930s photograph. Today the view is obscured by trees and of the sun-dial only the broken base remains.

155   Oxton Cricket Club is pictured in Townfield Lane in 1913. The club was founded here in 1875 and the main pavilion, which is almost unchanged today but is about to be extended, was erected in 1878. During the First World War no cricket was played, as vegetables and hay were grown here. The ground was purchased from the Earl of Shrewsbury in 1928 for £4,000 and in 1948 a site adjoining the 3rd XI ground for £445.

156   Looking along Bidston Road, *c.*1906, Silverdale Road is to the left of the trap and the smaller building above it being the *Carnarvon Castle Hotel*. All the buildings on the left except St Saviour's Church were destroyed by enemy action in August 1941, with the present pub being built on the site in 1956. The cottages across the road on the right, which were the cause of a bottle-neck, were demolished and the road was widened (*see* plate 157).

157 Looking down Bidston Road in the 1930s, Townfield Road is on the left and opposite is St Saviour's Church seen beyond Gerald Road. Oxton became a parish in 1851 when the first church was built on this site. Prior to that Oxton was part of Woodchurch parish but the church was not easily accessible. The church seen here replaced the original one in 1891. The car is parked outside the original *Carnarvon Castle* (*see* plate 156).

158 The shops seen in Rose Mount in the 1920s are from left: Herbert Rowlands, poulterer; Arthur Rowlands, fruiterer; Misses Selves, confectioner; J.S. Cooke, boot repairer (note the boot above the shop); F. Tutty, ironmonger; Miss White, milliner; J. Fletcher, grocer; Bertha Young, draper; Miss M. Crowhurst, confectioner; Mrs. M. Jones, greengrocer; Miss M. Wharton, dairy; Mrs. E. Parker, newsagent and Mrs. C. Cameron, confectioner. The five single-storied shops to the right of the car had been added onto existing houses.

159 This view looking up Woodchurch Lane was taken *c.*1910, when this was the main shopping area in the vicinity. Due to an increased demand from a growing population at the turn of the century, houses were converted into shops; also single-storied shops were built onto the front of existing houses, as seen on the right. Due to modern shopping trends, the majority of shops have since ceased trading and some have been converted back into houses.

160 Tramcar No. 57 is seen proceeding down Prenton Road West in 1907, with the terminus being at the top of this road before its junction with Storeton Road. This route opened 27 September 1901 with the double track seen here, which also ran along Borough Road, being increased from single track in 1906. In later years Football Special trams for Tranmere Rovers football club would park the length of this road on match day.

161 St Stephen's Church is pictured in Prenton Lane at its junction with Reservoir Road in the 1920s. The church, which was dedicated in 1897, cost £10,000 to build and seated 620 persons. Originally it was planned to erect a tower and spire but, due to lack of funds and rising costs, they were never built.

162 The Prenton War Memorial, seen standing in its own gardens in 1927, was erected in 1919 as a memorial to the people of Prenton who gave their lives during the First World War. It had to be reconstructed following bomb damage during the Second World War. Hillside, the house pictured side-on in Prenton Lane, was also destroyed by enemy action and a new house was built on the site. The house beyond, Halfryn, is still there today.

163 Northwood Road Primary School, Prenton is pictured in the 1950s. The school opened in 1954, being occupied by Woodchurch Road Junior School until 1957, while their bomb-damaged building was being repaired. Then in May 1957, the junior and infant departments took possession of the building. In 1971, when education in Birkenhead was reorganised, the junior department was designated a middle school, reverting back in 1983.

164 This view looking up Swan Hill, Woodchurch Road, Prenton was taken in 1927. The houses pictured, which were erected in 1890 and are still there today, were not lived in when built as it was then the practice not to move in for several years until the plaster had dried out. The posting box, which can be seen in the wall on the left, was moved across the road some years ago, and behind the wall is the *Swan Hotel* and bowling green (*see* plate 166).

165 The houses viewed on the right, which are still there today, can be seen in the previous picture, looking in the other direction. In the mid-1920s Birkenhead Co-op built a dairy on the site to the right and operated from there until the mid-1980s, with Swan Motors opening in 1988. The road has since been widened and Swan Court flats were built on the left *c.*1965. Residential buildings now occupy some of the fields in the background.

166 The *Swan Hotel* is pictured in Holm Lane in the 1920s when the publican was William Johnson. The pub dates back to at least 1890 when it was called the *White Swan.* The bowling green, which also dates back to at least 1890, is through the entrance on the right. The present building, which was opened *c.*1937, replaced the old hotel which was then demolished. The new pub is unusual in that all the corners of the building are rounded.

167 There has been a parish church of Holy Cross, Woodchurch, on this site since Saxon times, with parts of the present church representing the 12th, 14th, 16th and 20th centuries. Some of the areas that the ancient parish of Woodchurch covered included Oxton, Prenton, Noctorum and parts of Claughton. This church, which was the centre of a rural community until after the Second World War, is now part of a large housing estate (*see* plate 172).

168 A group of men posing in front of a smithy in Woodchurch prior to the First World War, when Thomas Lee was the blacksmith and a directory of 1850 records that a Thomas Lee (probably related) was the then blacksmith. By 1915 Joseph and Thomas Lee were trading as Automobile, Mechanical and General Engineers and by the 1920s they were also selling petrol. The building was demolished by 1936 and the site is now part of the *Arrowe Park Hotel*'s car park.

169 The *Horse and Jockey* inn at Woodchurch dates back to at least 1850 when the victualler was William Inglefield, who was also a wheelwright. When this photograph was taken *c.*1920, Septimus Broster was the victualler, who ran the pub from 1907 until he died in 1936. It was in that year that the *Arrowe Park Hotel* opened, taking the licence from the *Horse & Jockey*, which was then demolished.

170 Once probably a toll cottage in Church Lane, this small, ivy-covered building became the Woodchurch post office. In 1850 William Peilin was the sub postmaster when letters arrived from Birkenhead at 10.45a.m. and were despatched at 4.00p.m. This photograph was taken in 1915 when Edwin Pownall, who was the sub postmaster, was also a tailor. The cottage was demolished at the same time as other local buildings (*see* plates 168-9) and the roads were widened.

171 Church Terrace cottages in Pool Lane, which were believed to be over 200 years old and were owned by Woodchurch Parish Church, which they faced (*see* plate 167), are seen here in 1928. At that time George Mutch ran the shop on the left. The tenants of these cottages were rehoused when they were demolished in 1962 and Meadowside School was later built on the site.

172 These council houses, which are pictured in Ackers Road in the mid-1950s, were some of the 2,500 houses which were planned in the 1940s to be built on the new Woodchurch estate. The first house on this well designed, spacious estate, was formally opened on 6 May 1949. In 1933, the first Birkenhead & District Annual Sheep Dog Trials were held on Rectory Field, Woodchurch (now part of the estate).

H.R.H. THE PRINCE OF WALES AND SIR BADEN POWELL INSPECTING BOY SCOUTS.

173 This postcard was sold at the Arrowe Park International Scout Jamboree which took place from 31 July to 13 August 1929. The Prince of Wales is shown inspecting boy scouts with Lord Baden-Powell, the Chief Scout. This venue was chosen because 1929 was the 21st anniversary of the inaugural meeting of the Boy Scout Movement at Birkenhead Y.M.C.A. on 24 January 1908 (*see* plate 103).

174 This view of the Arrowe Park Jamboree was taken from an aeroplane over Woodchurch, with Thurstaston on the left horizon. The opening ceremony of the Pageant of Nations is in progress in front of the nine-section Grand Stand, specially erected for the Jamboree.

175 This was one of many postcard views of the Arrowe Park Jamboree taken by J. Woodhall of Grange Road, Birkenhead and depicts the Shropshire gateway on the right. The displays by the Shropshire Scouts included 'Old Shropshire', depicting ancient village life, camp craft, handicrafts, etc. Over 320,000 paying public visited the camp during the fortnight.

176 The Birkenhead Corporation bus No. 2 is seen passing Bidston Church, being one of 10 Leyland 'O' type 32-seater buses that were ordered in 1919. The destination sign reads 'Rock Ferry & Moreton'. The first service, which started on 12 July 1919, ran between Rock Ferry Pier and Park Station and was extended to Moreton Cross on 30 August 1919.

177 St Oswald's Church, Bidston, which is seen in Bidston Village at the turn of the century, was rebuilt in 1855-6 at a cost of £1,750 and the sanctuary was added in 1882. It was in this year that the church was dedicated, the name coming from an inscription on one of the bells which came from St Oswald's, Chester. There has been a church on this site probably from the 12th century; the present tower dates back to 1520.

178 The Y.M.C.A. Hut, pictured at Bidston, was used from the start of the First World War by the army, when Bidston became the site of a large training camp. This postcard was sent from a soldier at the Bidston camp in 1916 to his loved one; by 1917 the camp was used to house German prisoners of war. As a village hall it was later used for plays, jumble sales, coffee mornings, etc. It was burnt down some years ago.

179 This old school house at Bidston was built on land in School Lane donated by James Stanley in 1636. The left part of the building was for living accommodation and was added *c.*1810. A new school was erected in Bidston Village Road, opening on 13 August 1838. This building was destroyed by incendiary bombs on 12/13 March 1941 and two modern houses were later built on the site.

180 Many people in their 'Sunday best' are gathering around the windmill on Bidston Hill prior to the First World War. Birkenhead Corporation bought the 46-acre estate on Bidston Hill by public subscription and it was opened to the public as a recreational area from 1894 onwards. The hill is split in two by Vyner Road but linked by a steel bridge that spans it. This windmill dates back to the late 18th century (*see* plate 181).

181 Another view of Bidston windmill, taken in 1927 after the sails had been removed, having been damaged by gales; they were then replaced. The original mill, which dated back to at least 1596, was a wooden peg or post mill. The foundations of the mill, which was destroyed by fire in 1791, can be seen 20 miles north of the present brick mill that replaced it.

182 Bidston lighthouse, pictured here *c*.1910, had been rebuilt in 1872-3, the original one being erected for the Corporation of Liverpool in 1771. Behind the lighthouse, which was last used in 1913, is Bidston Observatory. This was opened in 1867, being operated by the Mersey Docks and Harbour Board. In 1929, the Board and Liverpool University combined to form the Liverpool Observatory and Tidal Institute, on which the Admiralty were represented.

183 Tam O'Shanter's Cottage is thought to date back to the 17th century. Its name comes from a scene from Robert Burns' poem *Tam O'Shanter*, on the left, which had been carved on the cottage by Richard Lea who was living here in 1837. The cottage was destroyed by fire in 1954 and again in 1974. However, it has been rebuilt as a working farm open to the public with an annual rent of a pine cone, payable to the Tam O'Shanter Trust, set up by the Birkenhead History Society.

184 The funeral procession for Private Tinsley is proceeding up Tollemache Road in 1914. He was killed when a stock shed, which was being used as a dormitory for the Bantam's Regiment, collapsed at the Bebington Showground (now The Oval). The cortège is passing Flaybrick Cemetery on the left and the large building in the centre is the Birkenhead Infectious Diseases Hospital which opened in 1894.

Bibliography

Abbott, E. Maurice, *History of the Diocese of Shrewsbury 1850-1986* (1987)

Allan, George A., *Birkenhead Park Football Club 1871-1921* (1921)

Allison, J.E., M.A., *Sidelights on Tranmere* (1976)

Aspinall, Henry K., *Birkenhead and its Surroundings* (1903)

Beazley, F.C., *Parish Church of St Saviour's, Oxton* (1930)

Bibby, C.L., *The Shaftes* (1974)

Bidston, Carol E., *Birkenhead in Times Past* (1978)

Bidston, Carol E., *Birkenhead of Yesteryear* (1985)

Boumphrey, Ian & Marilyn, *Yesterday's Wirral No. 2* (1981)

Boumphrey, Ian & Marilyn, *Yesterday's Wirral No. 7* (1992)

Bushell, W.F., M.A., *Guide to the Parish Church of Oxton*

Cammell Laird, *Builders of Great Ships* (1959)

Essington Fay, B., *On His Master's Service [Life of Charles Thompson]* (1904)

Fisher, Claude, *The World Jamboree* (1929)

Gamlin, Hilda, *Memories of Birkenhead* (1892)

Harden, D.M., *The Spire is Rising* (1983)

Heiser, H.B., *St Aidan's College, Birkenhead 1847-1947* (1947)

Kaighin, J.R., *Bygone Birkenhead* (1925)

McIntyre, W.R.S., *Birkenhead Yesterday and Today* (1948)

Malcolm, David, *Murder and Mayhem in Birkenhead* (1994)

Maund, T.B. & Jenkins, Martin, *The Tramways of Birkenhead and Wallasey* (1987)

Maund, T.B., *The Birkenhead Bus* (1994)

Maund, T.B., *The Wallasey Bus* (1995)

Merseyside Railway History Group, *Railway Stations of Wirral* (1994)

Mott, C.G., *Reminiscences of Birkenhead* (1900)

Neilson, H.B., *Auld-Lang-Syne* (1935)

Pevsner, N., & Hubbard, E., *The Buildings of England—Cheshire* (1971)

Stewart-Brown, R., *Birkenhead Priory and the Mersey Ferry* (1925)

Sulley, Philip, *History of Ancient and Modern Birkenhead* (1907)

Turvey, Rev. B.H.C., *Notes on the History of Woodchurch* (1953)

Turner, Tom, *Birkenhead Buses* (1978)

Upton, Gilbert, *Tranmere Rovers 1881-1921* (1991)

Woodhouse, W.E., *One in Heart [Birkenhead School 1860-1960]* (1960)

Young, Derek, *Pictures from the Past* (1979)

The following were also referred to:
Birkenhead Borough guides, souvenir booklets, newspaper articles, magazines, gazetteers of the time.

Index